Bond
No.1 for exam success

Verbal Reasoning

Assessment Practice for the 11+

Ages 6–7 Year 2

J M Bond & Jane Cooney

OXFORD
UNIVERSITY PRESS

Great Clarendon Street, Oxford, OX2 6DP, United Kingdom

Oxford University Press is a department of the University of Oxford.
It furthers the University's objective of excellence in research, scholarship,
and education by publishing worldwide. Oxford is a registered trade mark
of Oxford University Press in the UK and in certain other countries

© Oxford University Press 2025
Written by J M Bond and Jane Cooney
Illustrations © Oxford University Press 2025

The moral rights of the author have been asserted
Database right Oxford University Press (maker)

First published in 2025

All rights reserved. No part of this publication may be reproduced,
stored in a retrieval system, transmitted, used for text and data mining,
or used for training artificial intelligence, in any form or by any means,
without the prior permission in writing of Oxford University Press,
or as expressly permitted by law, or under terms agreed with the
appropriate reprographics rights organization. Enquiries concerning
reproduction outside the scope of the above should be sent to the
Rights Department, Oxford University Press, at the address above.

You must not circulate this book in any other binding or cover
and you must impose this same condition on any acquirer

British Library Cataloguing in Publication Data
Data available

978-1-38-206094-3

10 9 8 7 6 5 4 3 2 1

Printed in China

The manufacturing process conforms to the environmental
regulations of the country of origin

Acknowledgements

Content Development Editor and Reviewer: Anthea Morton
Page make-up: York Publishing Solutions Pvt. Ltd.
Cover illustrations: Lo Cole
Illustrations: York Publishing Solutions Pvt. Ltd.

Although we have made every effort to trace and contact
all copyright holders before publication this has not been
possible in all cases. If notified, the publisher will rectify
any errors or omissions at the earliest opportunity.

A Brief History of Bond

Bond 11+ has been the market leader in selective school admission test preparation since 1964, when J.M. Bond published her first book of practice tests.

Jean Moyra Bond was a school principal and passionate educator who started writing out practice questions for her pupils on slips of paper, to help get them test-ready, at a time when no formal resources were available. Her high-quality questions spawned a series of books and the Bond range grew from there; however their original author was advised to publish under her initials, rather than her name, as it was felt that the books would not sell as well if it was known they were written by a woman.

Happily, times have changed; but Jean Moyra Bond's legacy lives on, supporting thousands of pupils on their 11+ journey every year. 'J.M.' Bond was involved in writing and revising Bond materials up until her death in 2011, with the baton being passed on to the new generations of expert tutors who create Bond's peerless learning and practice content.

Now offering cutting-edge digital solutions, as well as a comprehensive print range, Bond remains as the gold standard in 11+ preparation to this day.

Contents

Welcome 4
A Note for Parents 4
How to Use This Book 4
Verbal Reasoning Skills 5

Learning Papers

1 Similar or Opposite 6
2 Picture Puzzles 10
3 Sequences and Patterns 16
4 Linking Words 21
5 The Alphabet 26
6 Making New Words 31
7 Letter Patterns 36
8 Sorting Sentences and Words 41
9 Anagrams 45
10 Symbols 49
Puzzle 1 54

Mixed Papers

Mixed Paper 1 57
Mixed Paper 2 60
Mixed Paper 3 63
Mixed Paper 4 66
Mixed Paper 5 69
Mixed Paper 6 72
Puzzle 2 76

Keywords 79
Answers A1
Progress Chart A10

Welcome

Bond's Verbal Reasoning resources provide thorough and continuous practice for key Verbal Reasoning skills. They are ideal preparation the 11+ and other selective school entrance exams.

Bond offers a complete, flexible programme of preparation materials that you can adapt to your child's specific needs. We provide a wide selection of question types and believes that an enriched education is the best preparation. We help children to both master the techniques and develop the logic and rationale to tackle any unknown question types.

KEY STUDY SKILLS

Here are some tips to help:

- Balance short bursts of practice with longer assessment papers.
- Create a quiet study space with pencils, an eraser and paper for working out.
- Limit distractions such as television, technology, and games.
- Remember that errors are useful – they are part of the journey to success.

A Note for Parents

Parents have a crucial role in helping children and motivating them. Here are some ways that you can really make a difference.

- Check your child is working at the right level. The goal is being able to score 85% on average. It is demotivating to them if they cannot complete questions.

- Mark work promptly and go through errors. If papers have not been marked, a child has no idea how they are doing or whether they are repeating the same mistakes.

- Limit the range of homework you give your child. The best results are achieved by a system that gradually increases in difficulty. Completing lots of books and papers does not guarantee your child's success and often creates stress.

- If your child is struggling with something specific, add additional support in that area.

- Communication is key. Encourage your child to focus on the positive.

How to Use This Book

It is very important you find the time to work through this book with your child. It is likely they will need support to understand the Key Skill explanations. Once these elements are understood the questions should be more easily accessed by them independently.

This book includes many step-by-step techniques for solving different question types.

- The first section of the book is the Learning Papers that focus on key skills with worked examples then questions for consolidation.

- The second section of the book is Mixed Papers so that children continue to consolidate and do not forget what they have learnt.

- There are fully worked-out answers to explain how an answer has been reached.

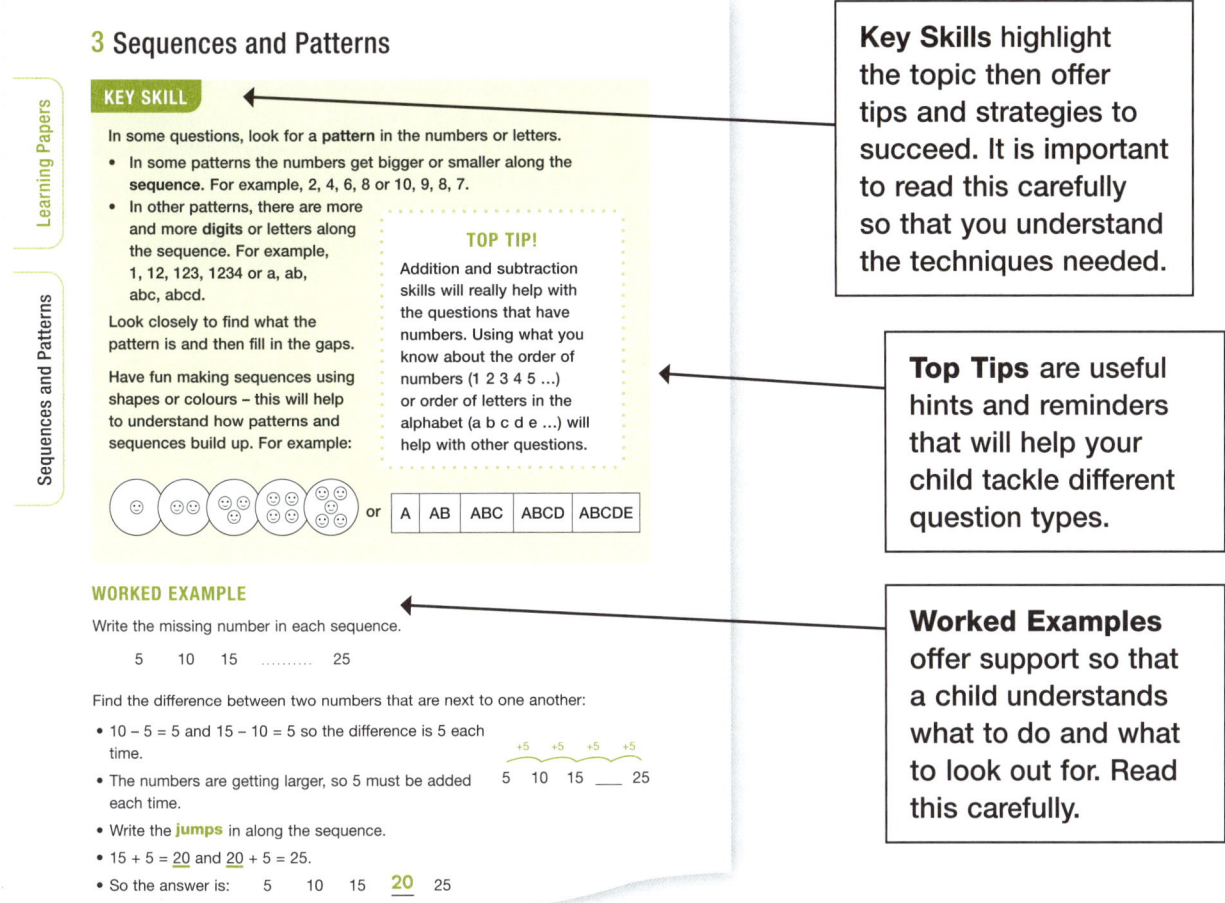

Key Skills highlight the topic then offer tips and strategies to succeed. It is important to read this carefully so that you understand the techniques needed.

Top Tips are useful hints and reminders that will help your child tackle different question types.

Worked Examples offer support so that a child understands what to do and what to look out for. Read this carefully.

Verbal Reasoning Skills

The Learning Papers cover key skills in similar and opposite meanings, picture puzzles, sequences and patterns, linking words, the alphabet, making new words, letter patterns, sorting sentences, anagrams and symbols appropriate for children of this age. Bond Assessment Practice draws on a wide variety of skills and question types so that children are always challenged to think and don't get bored of answering same question type repeatedly. These books help children 'think on their feet' and cope with the unexpected.

Do not forget that a rounded education is key. As well as testing skills, the 11+ requires children to possess a wide vocabulary and robust general knowledge.

- Read a range of literature with your child – stories, poems, non-fiction, comics – it all counts.

- Experience new places together such as a visit to a museum or a walk through the woods. New experiences can stimulate interesting discussions, deepen your child's understanding of the world, and help to build essential vocabulary.

- Play games together – card games, board games, and sudokus are all excellent ways of developing key skills such as logical reasoning and problem solving and expanding your child's vocabulary.

Learning Papers

1 Similar or Opposite

KEY SKILL

For these questions, the goal is to find words which have a **similar meaning** or the **opposite meaning**. For example:

- **Jump** has a similar meaning to **leap**.
- **Quiet** is the opposite of **loud**.

Try playing one of the following games to help (both are for two or more people):

Game 1:	Game 2:
The first person says a word. The next person has to say a word that is linked to it. Each word has to be linked to the one before in some way. For example: Person 1: **banana** Person 2: **yellow** Person 1: **green** Person 2: **grass**	Think of a word – but do not say it out loud. Say other words that are linked to the word in your head. The other person has to guess the word. When they do, swap roles.

TOP TIP!

Reading really helps with understanding lots of different types of words. This does not only have to be stories – comics, magazines and web pages help with this too.

WORKED EXAMPLE

Underline the word in the brackets **closest in meaning** to the word in capitals.

SMILE   (sulk   played   grin)

After reading the word in capitals, look at each of the words in brackets. Are there any that are similar or **mean the same**? Put the word in capitals into a sentence of your own to help with any difficult questions. For example:

The children SMILE happily.

- **The children sulk happily.**
  This does not make sense – someone is not happy when they sulk!
- **The children played happily.**
  The sentence makes sense, but the words have different meanings.
- **The children grin happily.**
  This makes sense and the meaning is similar, so this must be the answer:

    SMILE   (sulk   played   <u>grin</u>)

Now try it yourself!

Underline the word in the brackets **closest in meaning** to the word in capitals.

1 SHOE   (leg   boot   jumper)

2 GREAT   (huge   thin   empty)

3 RUSH   (hurry   slow   walk)

4 GLAD   (happy   mean   sorry)

5 RING   (circle   cross   square)

6 SHORT   (low   fat   tall)

7 PAIR   (shoes   four   two)

8 HUG   (bag   cuddle   cut)

Similar or Opposite

WORKED EXAMPLE

Underline the pair of words with the most similar meaning.

    happy, angry   begin, start   dear, read

- Look at the first pair of words and decide if they have a similar meaning.
- **Happy** and **angry** mean the opposite, so this cannot be the answer.
- Look at the second pair. **Begin** and **start** have a similar meaning, so this could be the answer.
- Check the last pair of words to be sure: **dear** and **read** have the same letters, but do not have the same meaning, so they cannot be the answer.
- This means that **begin** and **start** must be the answer, so underline them:

    happy, angry   <u>begin, start</u>   dear, read

Now try it yourself!

Underline the pair of words with the most similar meaning.

9	quick, fast	heavy, light	up, down	1
10	good, bad	dress, sock	near, close	1
11	run, fall	bad, awful	break, fix	1
12	sad, glad	cat, kitten	awake, asleep	1
13	chair, seat	meat, spoon	tea, cake	1
14	farm, school	red, mad	boat, ship	1
15	dog, cat	high, tall	wet, dry	1
16	pen, pencil	bed, book	walk, hot	1

WORKED EXAMPLE

Draw lines to match the pairs of words that have the opposite meaning. One has been completed as an example.

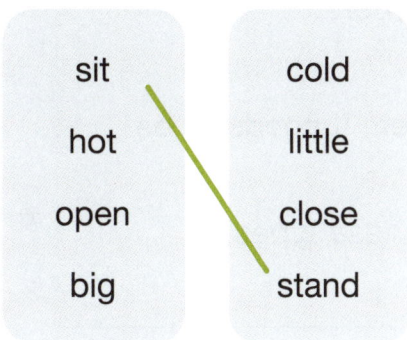

> **TOP TIP!**
> Start by reading through all the words. Match the easiest ones first. This will make the harder ones less tricky as there will be fewer words to choose from for the rest.

In this example, **sit** matches with **stand** because standing up is the opposite of sitting down.

Hot matches with **cold**, because when something is hot it is very warm, and when it is cold it is not warm. **Open** matches with **close** because if something is open, it is no longer closed. **Big** matches with **little** because big things are very large, and little things are very small.

Now try it yourself.

Draw lines to match the pairs of words that have the opposite meaning.

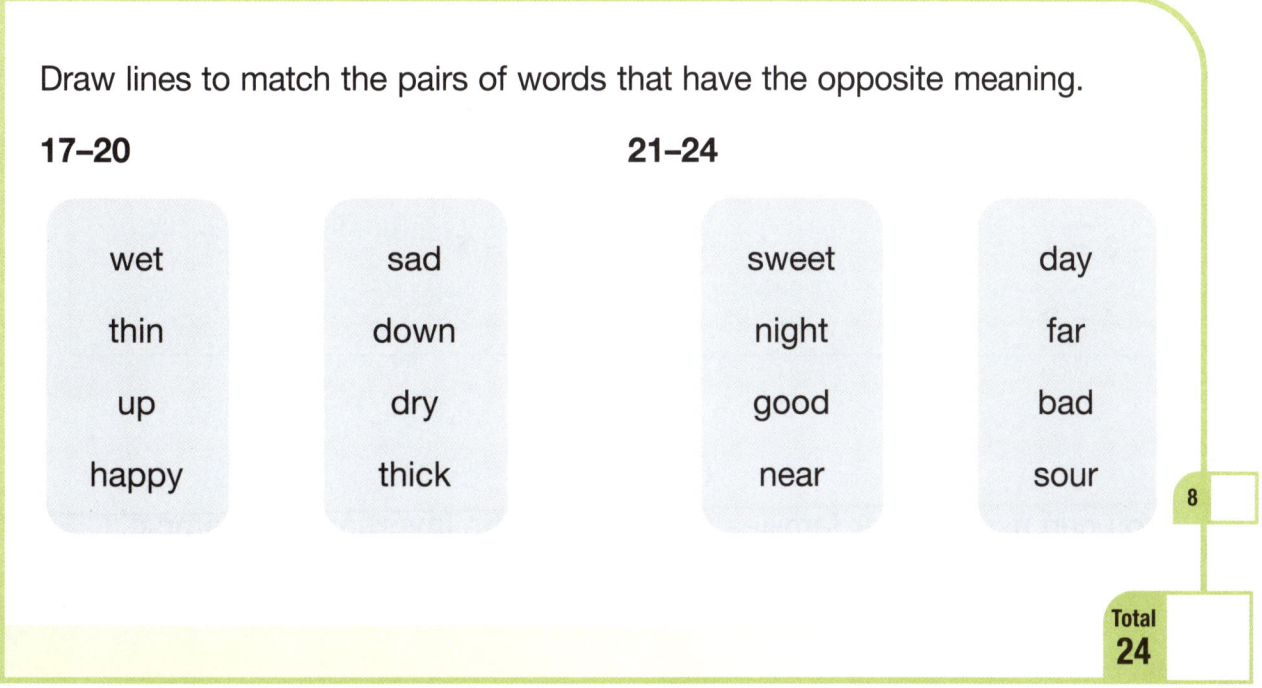

2 Picture Puzzles

KEY SKILL

In some questions, pictures are used instead of numbers.

- Find out what number the picture has replaced.
- The number the picture has replaced may be given. It needs to be used to solve a number sentence.

Learning how to complete **number families** makes these types of questions much easier. For example:

If 4 + 3 = 7,	If 2 × 5 = 10
then 3 + 4 = 7	then 5 × 2 = 10
Use this to write subtractions:	Use this to write divisions:
7 − 3 = 4	10 ÷ 2 = 5
and 7 − 4 = 3	and 10 ÷ 5 = 2
So the number family is:	So the number family is:
4 + 3 = 7	2 × 5 = 10
3 + 4 = 7	5 × 2 = 10
7 − 3 = 4	10 ÷ 2 = 5
7 − 4 = 3	10 ÷ 5 = 2

TOP TIP!

You can use number families to **complete the inverse**. For example, if 2 + 3 = 5, then 5 − 2 = 3.

Sometimes these questions will be written in words. The table shown will help with understanding and remembering what some of these words mean.

+ add altogether total	− difference take away less than
× multiply times	÷ divide share

WORKED EXAMPLE

Find the number the picture has replaced.

6 + 🐶 = 10   🐶 = ____

Write it out as a number family to help find the answer and look for the easiest one to complete.

| 6 + 🐶 = 10

 🐶 + 6 = 10

 (10 − 6 = 🐶)

 10 − 🐶 = 6 | 10 − 6 = 🐶 is the easiest one to complete here:

 10 − 6 = 4

 So the answer is: 🐶 = **4** |

TOP TIP!

Choose the **number sentence** from the number family that is easiest. Someone may find working out 20 ÷ 4 = 🐱 easier, but another person may find 🐱 × 4 = 20 easier.

Picture Puzzles

Try one with division.

20 ÷ 🐱 = 4   🐱 = ___

Written out as a number family this will be:

🐱 × 4 = 20	20 ÷ 4 = 🐱 is the same as 4 × 5 = 20
4 × 🐱 = 20	So the answer is: 🐱 = **5**
(20 ÷ 4 = 🐱)	
20 ÷ 🐱 = 4	

Now try it yourself!

Adding and Subtracting

Find the number the picture has replaced.

1. 8 + 🐶 = 10   🐶 = ...

2. 20 − 🐱 = 15   🐱 = ...

3. 🐰 + 3 = 7   🐰 = ...

4. 🐭 − 6 = 4   🐭 = ...

Multiplying and Dividing

Find the number the picture has replaced.

5. 2 × = 6   = ...

6. 15 ÷ = 5   🍐 = ...

7. 🍌 × 10 = 40   🍌 = ...

8.   ÷ 3 = 10   🍇 = ...

TOP TIP!

Practising times tables will help with questions on multiplication <u>and</u> division.

WORKED EXAMPLE

If ☺ = 1, 😂 = 2, 😀 = 3, find the **sum** of the following.

Write the answer as a number.

a) ☺ + 😂 = ...   b) 😂 + 😀 + ☺ = ...

In this question, each number is replaced with a picture. Write the number above the picture each time to find the number sentence to be solved.

a) 1 + 2 = 3
   ☺ + 😂

   So the answer is:
   ☺ + 😂 = **3**

b) 2 + 3 + 1 = 6
   😂 + 😀 + ☺

   So the answer is:
   😂 + 😀 + ☺ = **6**

Now try it yourself!

If 🌻 = 1, 🌸 = 2, 🌹 = 3, 🌷 = 4, find the sum of the following.

Write the answer as a number.

Example   🌻 + 🌸 = **3**

9   🌻 + 🌹 + 🌸 = ...   11   🌹 + 🌹 + 🌷 = ...

10   🌸 + 🌷 + 🌻 = ...   12   🌹 + 🌻 + 🌸 + 🌸 = ...

If ♪ = 1, 🎹 = 2, 🎧 = 3, 𝄞 = 4, 🎸 = 5, find the sum of the following.
Give the answer as a number.

13   ♪ + 🎧 + 𝄞 = ...   15   🎧 + 𝄞 + 🎸 = ...

14   🎸 + 🎹 + 🎹 = ...   16   🎹 + 🎧 + 🎹 + 🎧 = ...

WORKED EXAMPLE

For questions that use words and pictures, write out the number sentence or use number families.

Multiplication and Division

Double 🏉 = 16

🏉 = ...

To double means to multiply by 2:

2 × 🏉 = 16

🏉 × 2 = 16

16 ÷ 🏉 = 2

16 ÷ 2 = 🏉

16 ÷ 2 = 8

So the answer is: 🏉 = **8**

Half of ⚽ = 10

⚽ = ...

To halve means to divide by 2:

⚽ ÷ 2 = 10

20 ÷ 2 = 10

So the answer is: ⚽ = **20**

Addition and Subtraction

The **difference** between 10 and 4 is 🏓

🏓 = ...

Subtract to find the difference: 10 − 4 = 6

So the answer is: 🏓 = **6**

The sum of 7 and 🏆 = 11

🏆 = ...

7 + 🏆 = 11 and 7 + 4 = 11

So the answer is: 🏆 = **4**

Now try it yourself!

17 Double 🍒 = 20   🍒 = ... 1

18 Half of 🍉 = 7   🍉 = ... 1

19 The difference between 16 and 2 is 🎈   🎈 = ... 1

20 The sum of 10 and 🎺 is 19   🎺 = ... 1

21 Double 🚜 = 18   🚜 = ... 1

22 Half of 🐌 = 11   🐌 = ... 1

23 The difference between 18 and 6 is ☀️   ☀️ = ... 1

24 The sum of 12 and 🐟 is 20   🐟 = ... 1

Total 24

Picture Puzzles

15

3 Sequences and Patterns

KEY SKILL

In some questions, look for a **pattern** in the numbers or letters.

- In some patterns the numbers get bigger or smaller along the **sequence**. For example, 2, 4, 6, 8 or 10, 9, 8, 7.
- In other patterns, there are more and more **digits** or letters along the sequence. For example, 1, 12, 123, 1234 or a, ab, abc, abcd.

Look closely to find what the pattern is and then fill in the gaps.

Have fun making sequences using shapes or colours – this will help to understand how patterns and sequences build up. For example:

TOP TIP!
Addition and subtraction skills will really help with the questions that have numbers. Using what you know about the order of numbers (1 2 3 4 5 …) or order of letters in the alphabet (a b c d e …) will help with other questions.

 or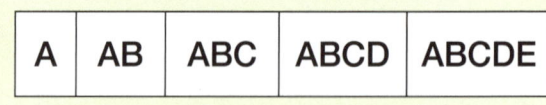

WORKED EXAMPLE

Write the missing number in each sequence.

    5   10   15   25

Find the difference between two numbers that are next to one another:

- 10 − 5 = 5 and 15 − 10 = 5 so the difference is 5 each time.
- The numbers are getting larger, so 5 must be added each time.
- Write the **jumps** in along the sequence.
- 15 + 5 = <u>20</u> and <u>20</u> + 5 = 25.
- So the answer is: 5   10   15   **20**   25

    +5 +5 +5 +5
5 10 15 ___ 25

Now try another one where the numbers get smaller.

50   40   20   10

- 50 − 40 = 10 and 20 − 10 = 10
- The numbers are getting smaller so 10 must be subtracted each time.
- Write the **jumps** in along the sequence.
- 40 − 10 = <u>30</u> and <u>30</u> − 10 = 20
- So the answer is: 50   40   **<u>30</u>**   20   10.

TOP TIP!
If the numbers get bigger, look for what has been added. If they get smaller, look for what has been taken away.

Now try it yourself.

Write the missing number in each sequence.

Example   5   10   15   **20**   25

1   2   4   6   10

2   1   3   5   9

3   12   11   9   8

4   8   6   5   4

5   0   10   30   40

6   3   7   9   11

7   12   10   6   4

8   3   6   9   15

WORKED EXAMPLE

Write the missing number in the sequence.   1   12   123   ....

In this sequence an extra digit is added each time.
Think about the order of numbers to help (1 2 3 4 5 6 7 8 and so on).

- The first part of the sequence is the digit **1**.
- The second part has 2 placed after the **1** to make **12**.
- The third part has 3 placed after the **12** to make **123**.

This means the next digit will be **4** and will be placed after **123**.

So the answer is: 1   12   123   **1234**

Give the next group of letters in each sequence. The alphabet has been written out to help.

a b c d e f g h i j k l m n o p q r s t u v w x y z

    a   ab   abc   ....

In this sequence an extra letter is added each time. Use the alphabet shown to help – the pattern will use the letters in the same order.

- The first part of the sequence is the letter **a**.
- The second part has **b** placed after the **a** to make **ab**.
- The third part has **c** placed after **ab** to make **abc**.

This means the letter will be **d** and placed after **abc**.

So the answer is: a   ab   abc   **abcd**

Now try it yourself.

Write the missing number in each sequence.

Example   1   12   123   **1234**

9   2   23   234   ....

10 3   34   345   ....

11 6   67   678   ....

12 23   234   2345   ....

Give the next group of letters in each sequence. The alphabet has been written out to help.

a b c d e f g h i j k l m n o p q r s t u v w x y z

Example   a   ab   abc   **abcd**

13   b   bc   bcd   ....

14   g   gh   ghi   ....

15   m   mn   mno   ....

16   p   pq   pqr   ....

17   j   jk   jkl   ....

18   w   wx   wxy   ....

Sequences and Patterns

WORKED EXAMPLE

Give the next **two** letters in each sequence. The alphabet has been written out to help.

a b c d e f g h i j k l m n o p q r s t u v w x y z

cd   ce   cf   ....

Sometimes one letter in the sequence might stay the same and another one might follow a different pattern.

- In each part of this sequence, the first letter stays the same: it begins with **c** each time.
- The second letter moves one place along the alphabet each time:

  d changes into **e** to make **ce**.

  e changes into **f** to make **cf**.

- This means the **f** will then change into **g** to make **cg**.
- So the answer is: cd   ce   cf   **cg**

19

Now try it yourself!

Give the next **two** letters in each sequence. The alphabet has been written out to help.

a b c d e f g h i j k l m n o p q r s t u v w x y z

Example   cd   ce   cf   **cg**

19   ab   ac   ad   ....

20   de   df   dg   ....

21   bb   bc   bd   ....

22   pq   pr   ps   ....

23   ac   ad   ae   ....

24   vw   vx   vy   ....

4 Linking Words

KEY SKILL

In some questions, the goal is to group words together. This could be because they have a similar meaning or they are linked in some way. For example:

- The words **huge**, **giant** and **large** can be grouped together as they all mean big.
- The words **chair**, **sofa** and **stool** can be linked together as they are all used for sitting.
- The word **cup** can be linked to **drink** as it is something you drink out of.

TOP TIP!

Have fun drawing pictures and writing any words that link to them. This will help you to find the different ways words can link together.

WORKED EXAMPLE

Write these words in the correct group.

girl   cat   man   lad   cow

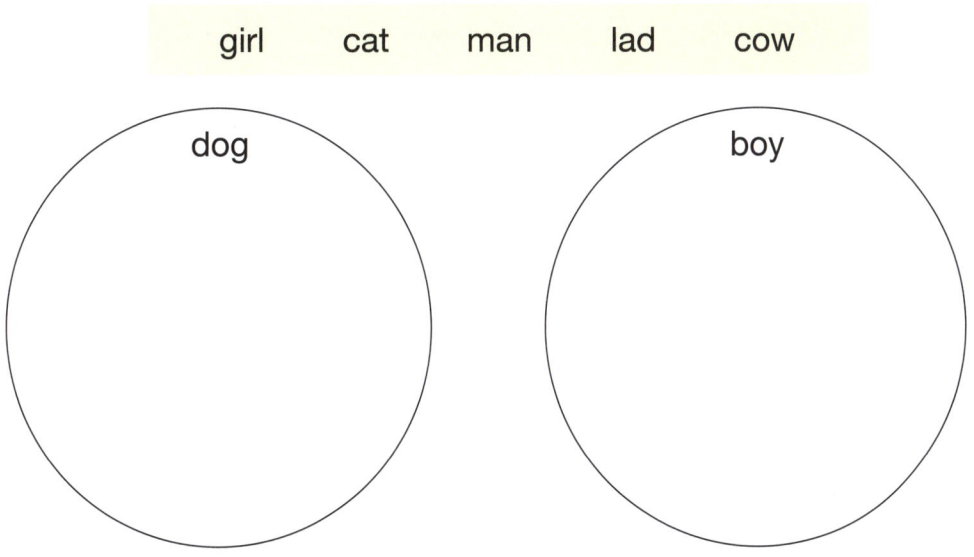

- Read through all the words in the list: **girl**, **cat**, **man**, **lad**, **cow**.
- Look at the titles of each group: **dog** and **boy**.
- Then, look at the first word in the list: **girl**. Decide which group it belongs in.
- A dog is an animal so it cannot be in this group! A girl is a type of person and so is a boy, so it must go in this group.
- Do the same with the rest of the words.

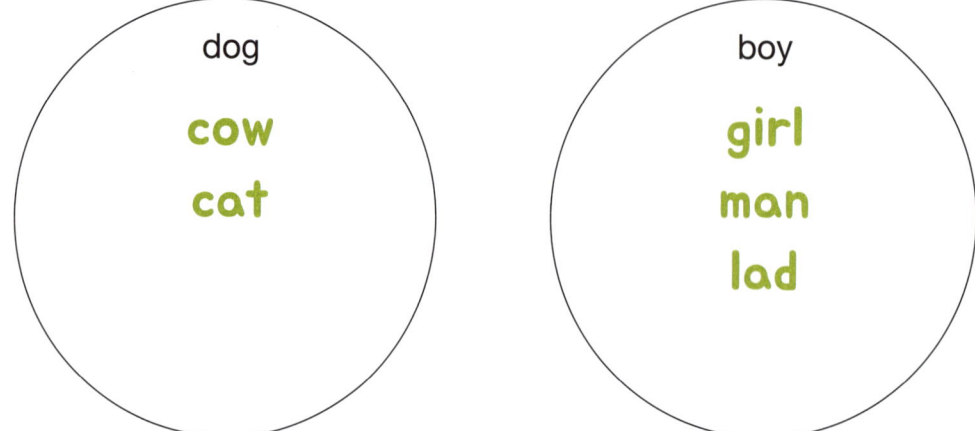

Now try it yourself.

1–5 Write these words in the correct group.

coat   pencil   crayon   hat   pen

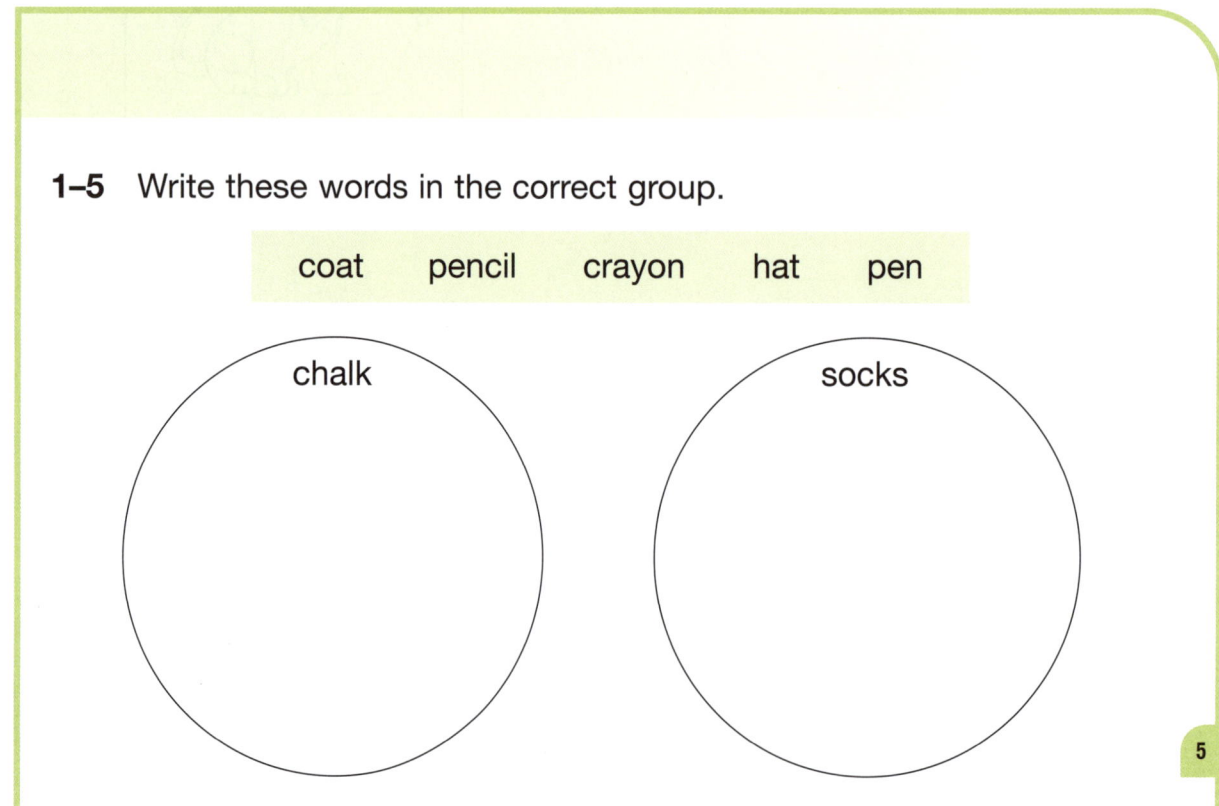

6–10

Write these words in the correct group.

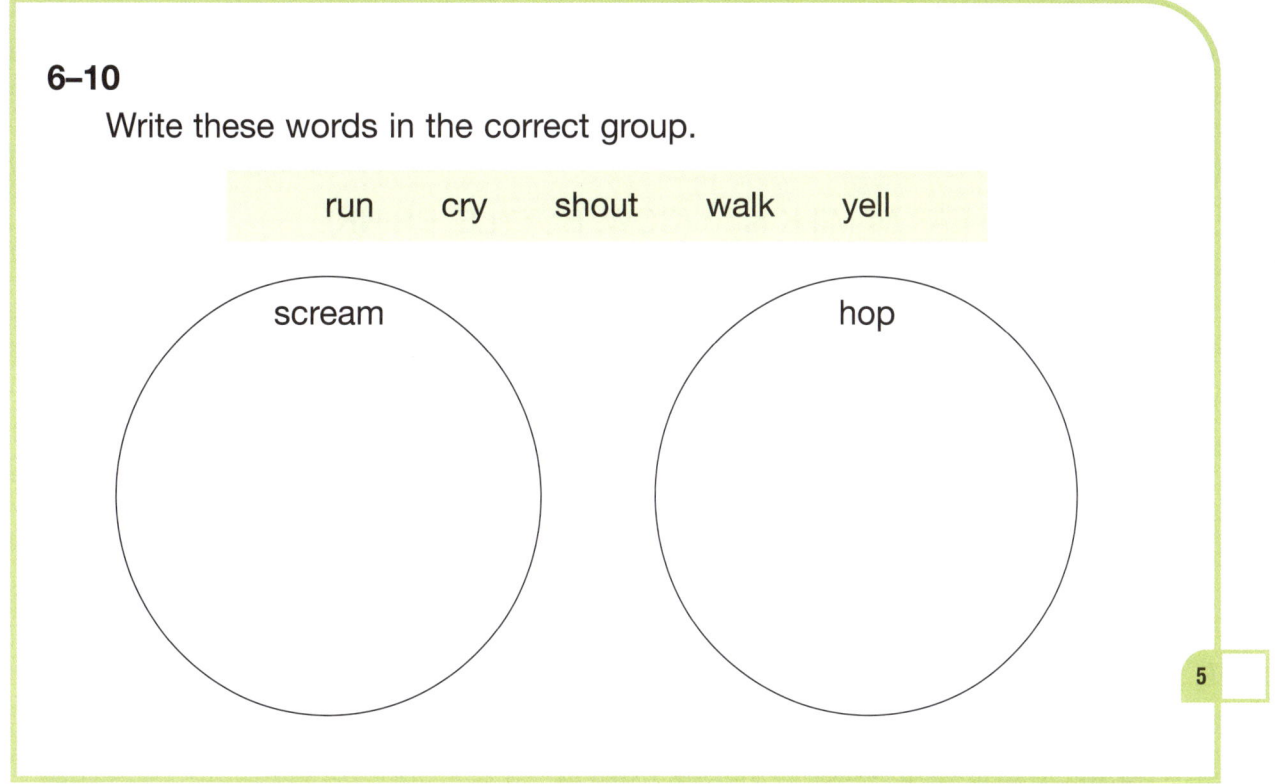

WORKED EXAMPLE

Match the second pair of words in the same way as the first pair. Underline the correct word in the brackets.

      HAND is to ARM as FOOT is to (HEAD, FINGER, LEG).

Look at the first two words in capital letters and think about how the words are linked:

- **HAND** and **ARM** are parts of the body that are joined to one another.
- The third word in CAPITALS is **FOOT** so look for a word that means a part of the body that joins to a foot.
- **HEAD** and **FINGER** are parts of the body, but they do not join to a foot!
- **LEG** is the answer, so underline it.

HAND is to ARM as FOOT is to (HEAD, FINGER, LEG).

Now try it yourself!

Linking Words

Match the second pair of words in the same way as the first pair. Underline the correct word in the brackets.

11 APPLE is to EAT as MILK is to (COW, BOTTLE, DRINK).

12 LAUGH is to HAPPY as CRY is to (SAD, GLAD, FUN).

13 BIRD is to FLY as FISH is to (WATER, SKY, SWIM).

14 PIG is to STY as MAN is to (HOUSE, BARN, TREE).

15 HAT is to HEAD as SOCK is to (SHOE, FOOT, SOFT).

16 TRIANGLE is to 3 as SQUARE is to (2, 4, 3).

17 ELEPHANT is to TRUNK as PIG is to (TUSK, SNOUT, TROTTER).

WORKED EXAMPLE

Underline the two words which are the **odd ones out** in the following groups of words.

    house   black   king   purple   green

- Read through all the words in the list first.
- Look at the first word. Does it have a similar meaning or is it linked in any way with the others?
- A **house** is a building or where someone lives. No other words have a similar meaning, so try the next word.
- **Black** is a colour and so are **purple** and **green**.

This means **black**, **purple** and **green** can be grouped together and **house** and **king** are the odd ones out.

So the answer is: <u>house</u>   black   <u>king</u>   purple   green

Now try it yourself!

Underline the two words which are the odd ones out in the following groups of words.

18	hat	gloves	silk	coat	cotton
19	tower	clock	watch	castle	fort
20	stair	flat	house	floor	cottage
21	leaf	flower	bench	pond	branch
22	TV	oven	shower	sink	bath
23	apple	orange	cake	pear	bread
24	line	ring	loop	space	hoop

5 The Alphabet

KEY SKILL

These types of questions use the **alphabet**. The alphabet is shown, but learning the order of the letters will really help. There are lots of fun ways of doing this:

- Make cards with groups of the letters from the alphabet on them, like the ones shown below.
- Muddle up the first few cards, then put them in order and check if it is right.
- Add another card, then muddle and put them in order again.
- Continue adding more and more cards. This will make finding the order of the letters in the alphabet will be much less tricky.

TOP TIP!

Learn a song! Lots of different ABC songs can be found on the internet to sing along to.

| ABC | DEFG | HIJ | KLMN | OPQ | RST | UVW | XYZ |

WORKED EXAMPLE

Make a word from the **2nd**, **5th** and **4th** letters of the alphabet. The alphabet has been written out to help.

a b c d e f g h i j k l m n o p q r s t u v w x y z

Count along the alphabet to find the letters in the question. The correct letters will spell out a word.

This table shows the first, second, third, fourth and fifth letters of the alphabet.

a	b	c	d	e
1st	2nd	3rd	4th	5th

Now let's try answering the question.

- The 2nd letter is **b**.
- The 5th letter is **e**
- The 4th letter is **d**.

Write them in the same order to find the answer: **bed**

Now try it yourself!

Make a word from the letters of the alphabet. The alphabet has been written out to help.

a b c d e f g h i j k l m n o p q r s t u v w x y z

1. Make a word from the 2nd, 5th and 7th letters of the alphabet.

   ....

2. Make a word from the 8th, 1st and 4th letters of the alphabet.

   ....

3. Make a word from the 2nd, 1st, 3rd and 11th letters of the alphabet.

   ....

4. Make a word from the 12th, 15th, 14th and 7th letters of the alphabet.

   ....

5. What word is made from the 2nd, 9th and 7th letters?

   ....

6. What word is made from the 8th, 5th, 1st and 4th letters?

   ....

7. What word is made from the 6th, 1st, 4th and 5th letters?

   ....

8. What word is made from the 3rd, 1st, 11th and 5th letters?

   ....

The Alphabet

WORKED EXAMPLE

Fill in the missing letters. The alphabet has been written out to help.

A B C D E F G H I J K L M N O P Q R S T U V W X Y Z

A is to B as C is to ___

- In this question, the goal is to find the pattern of how the letters change. Use the same pattern to find the missing letter.
- **A** is to **B** means the letter **A** has changed into **B** by moving forward one place along the alphabet.
- **C** is to ___ means that **C** changes in the same way by moving forward one place too.
- **D** is one place forward.

So the answer is: A is to B as C is to **D**

Let's try another example:

E is to H as J is to ___

- **E** is to **H** means the letter **E** has changed into **H** by moving forward three places along the alphabet.
- **J** is to ___ means that **J** changes in the same way by moving forward three places too.
- **M** is three places forward.

So the answer is: E is to H as J is to **M**

Now try it yourself!

Fill in the missing letters. The alphabet has been written out to help.

A B C D E F G H I J K L M N O P Q R S T U V W X Y Z

9 A is to B as D is to ___

10 A is to E as B is to ___

11 B is to C as G is to ___

12 L is to N as O is to ___

13 G is to I as H is to ___

14 C is to F as D is to ___

15 C is to H as B is to ___

16 B is to E as I is to ___

WORKED EXAMPLE

Write these words in **alphabetical order**. The alphabet has been written out to help.

a b c d e f g h i j k l m n o p q r s t u v w x y z

    truck   car   bus

(1) …………………… (2) …………………… (3) ……………………

Alphabetical order means the same order as letters in the alphabet. Look at the first letter of each word and find which one comes first in the alphabet.

- The word **truck** begins with **t**.
- The word **car** begins with **c**.
- The word **bus** begins with **b**.

Look at where the letters **t**, **c** and **b** are in the alphabet:

a ⓑ ⓒ d e f g h i j k l m n o p q r s ⓣ u v w x y z

The first letter that has been circled is **b**, so this means the word **bus** must be first. The next letter is **c**, so the word **car** must be next. The last letter to be circled is **t**, so the word **truck** must be last. So the answer is:

    truck   car   bus

(1) **bus** (2) **car** (3) **truck**

Now try it yourself!

Write these words in alphabetical order. The alphabet has been written out to help.

a b c d e f g h i j k l m n o p q r s t u v w x y z

17 cap   pat   hat

(1) .... (2) .... (3) ....

18 man   can   fan

(1) .... (2) .... (3) ....

19 let   met   jet

(1) .... (2) .... (3) ....

20 fed   bed   wed

(1) .... (2) .... (3) ....

21 day   way   say

(1) .... (2) .... (3) ....

22 hit   sit   bit

(1) .... (2) .... (3) ....

23 wet   set   get

(1) .... (2) .... (3) ....

24 joy   toy   boy

(1) .... (2) .... (3) ....

Total 24

6 Making New Words

> **KEY SKILL**
>
> These types of questions might need:
> - a letter is added to make a new word
> - another word added to make a new word
> - a letter removed to make a new word.
>
> Think about **letter patterns** within words (these are also called **digraphs** and **trigraphs**). For example, _tch, _ck or _ea_. Turn this into a fun game by making some cards like the ones shown below.
>
> - Mix them up and then choose one at random.
> - Write down all the different words that can be made using the letters on the card.
> - Keep score and then try to beat your best one!
>
> | _DGE | _NK | _TCH | _ISH | _CK |
>
> For example, the chosen card could be:
>
> | _NK |
>
> Words that can be made using this are: drink, link, stink, think, thank, sank, bank, bunk ... and so on.
>
> How many more can you find?

WORKED EXAMPLE

Remove one letter from the word in capital letters to leave a new word. The meaning of the new word is given in the clue.

    A U N T   an insect   ....

- Look at the clue first and think about possible answers. For example, an insect could be: **BEE**, **ANT** or **FLY**.
- Then look at the word in capitals. Can any of the letters be removed to make one of the possible answers?
- **U** can be removed from **AUNT** to make the word **ANT**.

So the answer is: A U N T   an insect   **ANT**

Now try it yourself!

Remove one letter from the word in capital letters to leave a new word. The meaning of the new word is given in the clue.

> **TOP TIP!**
> The order of letters in capitals does not change – a letter or word is only added or removed!

1 COST   a baby's bed   ....

2 TALL   everyone   ....

3 BLOW   the opposite of 'high'   ....

4 ROAD   a kind of stick   ....

5 FROG   a mist   ....

6 DRAW   not cooked   ....

7 MATE   a small kind of rug   ....

8 BOUT   the opposite of 'in'   ....

WORKED EXAMPLE

Add one letter from the list to the front of the capital letters. The sentences must make sense. Each letter can only be used once.

B   L   C

1   I drink from a _____UP.

2   I hurt my _____EG playing football.

3   We went to the _____ANK to get some money.

- Try each of the letters before **UP** in the first question: BUP, CUP and LUP.
- BUP and LUP are not real words so cannot be the answer.
- Only **CUP** is a real word and the sentence makes sense as a cup can be drunk from.
- Cross the C out to see which letters are left to use.
- Then try the letters that are left over in the next question: BEG and LEG
- BEG is a real word, but 'I hurt my BEG playing football' does not make sense!
- LEG must be the answer here.
- Check the last letter makes sense in the last question: 'We went to the BANK to get some money.'
- So the answer is:
    1 I drink from a **C**UP.
    2 I hurt my **L**EG playing football.
    3 We went to the **B**ANK to get some money.

Now try it yourself.

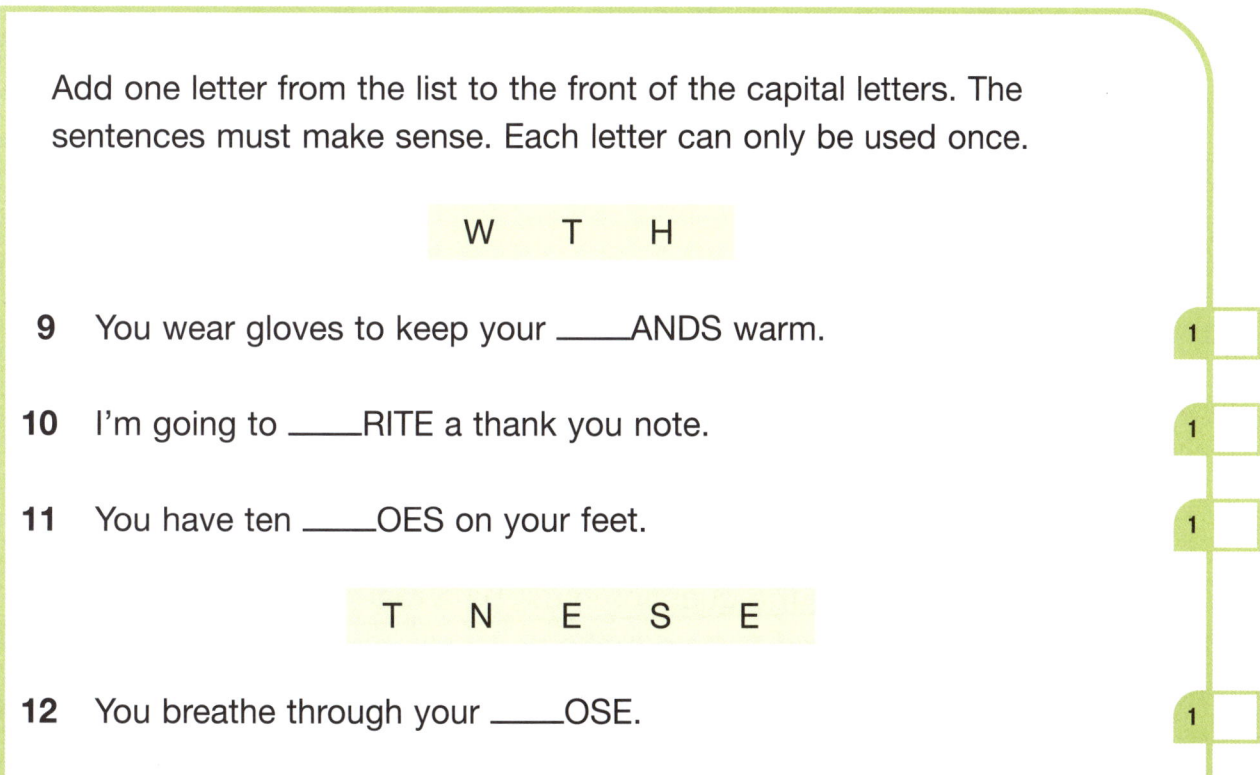

Add one letter from the list to the front of the capital letters. The sentences must make sense. Each letter can only be used once.

W   T   H

9   You wear gloves to keep your ____ANDS warm.

10 I'm going to ____RITE a thank you note.

11 You have ten ____OES on your feet.

T   N   E   S   E

12 You breathe through your ____OSE.

13 You hear with your ____ARS. 1

14 Your ____LBOW is part of your arm. 1

15 ____REES grow in forests and in gardens. 1

16 When it is warm we like to ____WIM in the pool. 1

WORKED EXAMPLE

Choose a word from the list that can be put in front of all of the following words to form new words. Each one must be a real word.

| sky | wind | sun | air |

.... shine   .... set

.... burn   .... glasses

Try each of the words in the list with the words in the question:

- Skyshine, skyset, skyburn and skyglasses are not real words, so try another word from the list.

- Sunshine, sunset, sunburn and sunglasses are all real words, so 'sun' must be the answer:

sunshine   **sun**set   **sun**burn   **sun**glasses

TOP TIP!

Remember: every word in the question must be a real word! For example, 'foot' can be used to help make 'football', but it does not work in front of all of the other words – try another word from the list if this happens.

Now try it yourself!

17–20

Choose a word from the list that can be put in front of all of the following words to form new words. Each one must be a real word.

foot   snow   hill   road

.... flake

.... ball

.... man

.... drop

20–24

glass   book   door   chair

.... knob

.... bell

.... mat

.... step

Making New Words

7 Letter Patterns

KEY SKILL

These questions are about making new words by changing or adding letters. Practising spelling really helps, or have a go at creating letter chains. For example:

- Start with the word BUT.
- Change the U to E to make the word BET.
- Then change the B to P to make the word PET.
- Then change the T to N to make the word PEN and so on.
- BUT → BET → PET → PEN → ?

This is just one example – this can be done in lots of different ways. For example, the U in BUT could be changed to A instead to make BAT and so on.

Here are some other words to use as starting points:
BEE, TON or CAP

Have a go at making the chain longer each time – make it as long as possible!

TOP TIP!

Think about different **letter patterns** and try changing the first letter. For example:

Start with the letter pattern '___ one' and add different letters to the front to make different words. For example, 'bone', 'done', 'gone' and 'tone' – there are many more!

Here are a couple of other letter patterns: '___ ake', '___ ine' and '___ all'. Some letter patterns will have more words than others – which has the most?

WORKED EXAMPLE

Change the first word of the third pair in the same way as the other pairs to give a new word.

    DIG, DOG   FIG, FOG   BIG, ...

- Look at the first pair of words:
- The middle letter in **DIG** has changed from **I** to **O** to make the word **DOG**.
- Check the second pair of words to see if the pattern is the same:
- The middle letter in **FIG** has changed from **I** to **O** to make the word **FOG**.

This means the middle letter in **BIG** will change from **I** to **O** as well, making the word **BOG**.

So the answer is:

    DIG, DOG   FIG, FOG   BIG, **BOG**

Now try it yourself!

Change the first word of the third pair in the same way as the other pairs to give a new word.

1 WET, WIT   SET, SIT   PET, ...

2 NET, NUT   PET, PUT   BET, ...

3 BIN, BAN   TIN, TAN   PIN, ...

4 GET, GOT   LET, LOT   NET, ...

5 CAN, CAT   FAN, FAT   BAN, ...

6 DAB, DUB   CAB, CUB   TAB, ...

7 SET, SAT   BET, BAT   MET, ...

8 JET, JOT   NET, NOT   PET, ...

Letter Patterns

WORKED EXAMPLE

Change the first word into the last word, by changing one letter at a time. The word in the middle must be a real word.

IS → .... → OF

In these questions, one letter changes in the first word to make the middle word. Then one letter changes in the middle word to make the last word. Use the letters in the words shown to help.

- Try changing the first letter in **IS** into the first letter in **OF**:
  IS becomes **OS** – this isn't a word so cannot be the answer.
- Try changing the second letter in **IS** to the second letter in **OF**:
  IS becomes **IF** – this is a real word so it must be the answer.
- IS → **IF** → OF

Now try it yourself!

Change the first word into the last word, by changing one letter at a time. The word in the middle must be a real word.

Example   IS → **IF** → OF

9   UP → .... → IS

10 AM → .... → IT

11 AS → .... → IF

12 HE → .... → BY

13 US → .... → IT

14 AN → .... → IF

15 BY → .... → WE

16 AT → .... → ON

WORKED EXAMPLE

Add one letter from the list to the end of the first word and start of the second word. Each letter can only be used once.

> y g n

1 fro (____) rass
2 pla (____) ellow
3 moo (____) ote

Try a letter with the words in the first question:
- **froy** and **yrass** are not real words, so that cannot be the answer.
- **frog** and **grass** are both real words, so this must be the first answer.

Then try one of the letters that are left over with the words in the second question:
- **plan** is a word but **nellow** is not a word, so that cannot be the answer.
- **play** and **yellow** are both real words, so this must be the second answer.

Check that the letter remaining makes two more words:
- **moon** and **note** are both real words so this must be the third answer.

So the answer is:
  fro (**g**) rass
  pla (**y**) ellow
  moo (**n**) ote

Now try it yourself.

Add one letter from the list to the end of the first word and start of the second word. Each letter can only be used once.

> w t d k

17 fin (____) raw

18 che (____) est

19 mar (____) ey

20 boa (____) rip

d   e   t   n

21 wis (____) lse

22 bes (____) rue

23 bir (____) usty

24 brow (____) ose

TOP TIP!

Practising spelling skills helps with this type of question – there are lots of apps that make learning to spell fun!

8 Sorting Sentences and Words

> ### KEY SKILL
>
> In some questions, the goal is to choose the correct words to get a sentence to make sense or to form a new word. Try writing some sentences and then changing them into silly ones! This is a fun way to help understand which types of words can change in these questions.
>
> Write a simple sentence first, then change one word:
>
> For example:
>
> > The mouse <u>squeaked</u> when it saw the cheese.
>
> could be changed into:
>
> > The mouse <u>roared</u> when it saw the cheese.
>
> You can also have fun drawing a picture of the silly thing that is happening!

ROAR!!

WORKED EXAMPLE

Underline one word from the brackets so that the sentences make sense.

> The (car, cow, table) was eating grass.

- Read the whole of the sentence first to get an idea of what it is about:

  The sentence is about something eating grass.

- Try the first word in the brackets:

  The **car** was eating grass does not make sense, so this cannot be the answer!

- Try the next word in the brackets:

  The **cow** was eating grass makes sense, so this could be the answer.

- Try the last word in the brackets to be sure:

  The **table** was eating grass does not make sense so this cannot be the answer!

So, the answer is: The **cow** was eating grass.

Now try it yourself!

Underline one word from the brackets so that the sentences make sense.

1. They sat down on a (lamp, seat, wave).
2. She cooked some (ice-cream, rice, car).
3. The cat ate its (wood, dish, food).
4. He put the book on the (table, oven, water).
5. The stars were in the (dress, sky, box).
6. She wore a (coat, cat, cow) as she was cold.
7. We had (floor, flower, fish) for our supper.
8. We walked to the park to play (football, swimming, reading).
9. The car was in the (rug, garage, cloud).

WORKED EXAMPLE

Find and underline the two words which need to change places for each sentence to make sense.

She went to letter the write.

- Read the whole sentence first to get an idea of what it is about:
  It is about a someone, a letter and writing.

- Read through the sentence again to find where it begins to not make sense:
  She went to letter doesn't make sense. So **letter** must be one of the words that needs to swap.

- Look at the remaining words and try swapping the word 'letter' with them:
  She went to the letter write – this does not make sense!
  She went to write the letter – this makes sense so it must be the answer.

So the answer is: She went to write the letter.

Now try it yourself!

Find and underline the two words which need to change places for each sentence to make sense.

10 The water in the cold pool was too swimming. □1

11 The flat stop is two streets from our bus. □1

12 The dog barked all long day. □1

13 The fence jumped over the horse. □1

14 The cheese ate all of the mice. □1

15 We all town into walked. □1

16 I cakes made for the party. □1

17 Ravi friend's to his rode house. □1

18 I can fast very run. □1

> **TOP TIP!**
>
> Write a sentence on a piece of paper, then cut out each word. Muddle up the words and then read them – have fun making silly sentences! What is the silliest one?

WORKED EXAMPLE

Match one word from the group on the left with one word from the group on the right to form a new word. The word on the left always comes first.

sun	berry
straw	yard
farm	flower

.... + ... = ...

.... + ... = ...

.... + ... = ...

- Choose one word from the group on the left and try it with each of the words in the group on the right: **sun** + **berry** = **sunberry**, **sun** + **yard** = **sunyard** and **sun** + **flower** = **sunflower**.
- Only **sunflower** is a real word, so this must be one of the answers.
- Cross the words **sun** and **flower** out so it is clear which words are left.
- Choose another word from the ones on the left and try it with each of the remaining words on the right: **farm** + **berry** = **farmberry** and **farm** + **yard** = **farmyard**.
- Only **farmyard** is a real word, so this must be another answer.
- This leaves **straw** + **berry**, which makes the word **strawberry**.

So the answer is:

sun + flower = sunflower
farm + yard = farmyard
straw + berry = strawberry

Now try it yourself!

Match one word from the group on the left with one word from the group on the right to form a new word. The word on the left always comes first.

19–21

.... + ... = ...

.... + ... = ...

.... + ... = ...

suit	stool
toad	case
star	fish

22–24

.... + ... = ...

.... + ... = ...

.... + ... = ...

foot	brush
tooth	ground
play	ball

Total **24**

9 Anagrams

KEY SKILL

These questions are all about **anagrams**. Anagrams are where the letters in words are muddled up.

In some questions, the goal is to find the letters of one word in another word. For example:

- Some of the letters in the word **window** can be used to make the word **down** (W I N D O W).
- Some of the same letters are used, but they are in a different order.

In some questions, all of the letters are used to form new words. For example:

- The word 'are' is made up of the same letters as the word **ear**.

In other questions, the goal is to put the muddled letters in the correct order to find the answer in a sentence. For example:

A BEZAR is an animal with stripes. ....

- Use the clues in the sentence to help find the word ZEBRA.

Have fun drawing and colouring the different letters of the alphabet. Cut each letter out and see how many different words can be made.

For example, the words **bead**, **beat** and **date** can be made from the following letters.

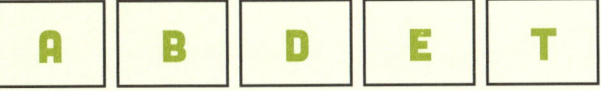

WORKED EXAMPLE

Underline the one word which <u>cannot be made</u> from the letters of the word in capital letters.

    G R O W N   now   worn   worm   won

Look at each word and cross off each letter that is also in the word GROWN.

    n̶o̶w̶   w̶o̶r̶n̶   w̶o̶r̶m   w̶o̶n̶

Look at the words and circle any letters that are not crossed out.

    n̶o̶w̶   w̶o̶r̶n̶   w̶o̶r̶(m)   w̶o̶n̶

The only word that does not have the same letters is **worm**, so it cannot be made from the word in capital letters.

So the answer is:

G R O W N   now   worn   <u>worm</u>   won

TOP TIP!

There should be only one word that does not have all the same letters as the one in capitals. If there are more check again to see if any of the circled letters are in the word in capitals after all!

Now try it yourself!

Underline the one word which <u>cannot be made</u> from the letters of the word in capital letters.

1	PARTY	rat	try	pay	arm
2	WHEAT	tea	the	bat	wet
3	HOLIDAY	aid	lid	had	dip
4	DREAD	dad	red	and	are
5	TABLE	tea	lap	bat	let
6	HOTEL	let	toe	hot	eat
7	HEATING	hat	get	ear	tea
8	FATHER	the	rat	fur	tar

WORKED EXAMPLE

Underline the two words which are made from the same letters.

  TAP   PET   TEA   POT   EAT

- Read through each of the words first.
- Look at the first word in the list: **TAP**. Check if it has the same letters as any of the other words.
- There are no other words made up of the letters **T**, **A** and **P**, so move onto the next word.
- There are no other words made up of the letters **P**, **E** and **T**, so move onto the next word.
- The word **TEA** has the same letters as **EAT**, so this must be the answer:

  TAP   PET   <u>TEA</u>   POT   <u>EAT</u>

Now try it yourself!

Underline the two words which are made from the same letters.

9	NIP	PEN	PUN	PIN	PAN
10	KIT	INK	KEN	NUT	KIN
11	BEG	BUG	GAS	BAG	SAG
12	NOT	NUT	TEN	TON	TAN
13	TAB	TUB	NIB	NAB	BIN
14	PIT	TOP	PUT	TIP	PAT
15	PUT	PAT	TOP	PET	TAP
16	BID	BUD	BAD	DAB	BED

WORKED EXAMPLE

The letters of the word in capitals have been muddled up. Put them in the correct order to make a proper word. The answer will complete the sentence sensibly.

A BEZAR is an animal with stripes. ....

- Read through the whole sentence to get an idea of what it is about.
- It is about an animal with stripes.
- Think about animals that have stripes: a tiger and a zebra have stripes.
- Only **zebra** has the same letters as BEZAR, so this must be the answer:

A BEZAR is an animal with stripes. **ZEBRA**

Now try it yourself!

The letters of the word in capitals have been muddled up. Put them in the correct order to make a proper word. The answer will complete the sentence sensibly.

17 LEBU is my favourite colour. .... [1]

18 The CKDU quacked as it swam in the pond. .... [1]

19 The birds have made a nest in a EERT in our garden. .... [1]

20 I went to DBE as I was tired. .... [1]

21 I like it when the NSU is out. .... [1]

22 I took my OGD for a walk. .... [1]

23 Kate wears her TAH when it is hot. .... [1]

24 The rain fell from the KYS and I got wet. .... [1]

Total **24**

10 Symbols

> ### KEY SKILL
>
> These questions are all about using **symbols**. They could show:
>
> - letters that have been replaced with symbols
> - letters that have been replaced with numbers
> - numbers replaced with letters.
>
> It is a fun way to improve your maths and problem-solving skills. Symbols are everywhere and mean lots of different things. Some examples are shown here:
>
>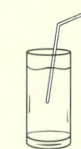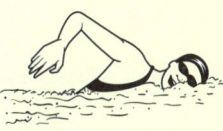
>
> tent   drink   castle   swimming   woods or forest
>
> ### TOP TIP!
>
> Have fun drawing symbols or pictures that have a hidden meaning. For example, the following picture could mean that people need to be quiet because a cat is sleeping!
>
>

WORKED EXAMPLE

In a code, **READ** is written as   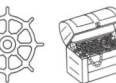 [treasure chest symbol]

What word is   [anchor] the code for? ....

- Each letter has been replaced by a symbol:
  - [ship] = R
  - [anchor] = E
  - [wheel] = A
  - [chest] = D

- The first symbol is ⚙ so the first letter is A.
- The second symbol is ⛵ so the second letter is R.
- The third symbol is ⚓ so the third letter is E.

So the answer is: **ARE**

Now try it yourself.

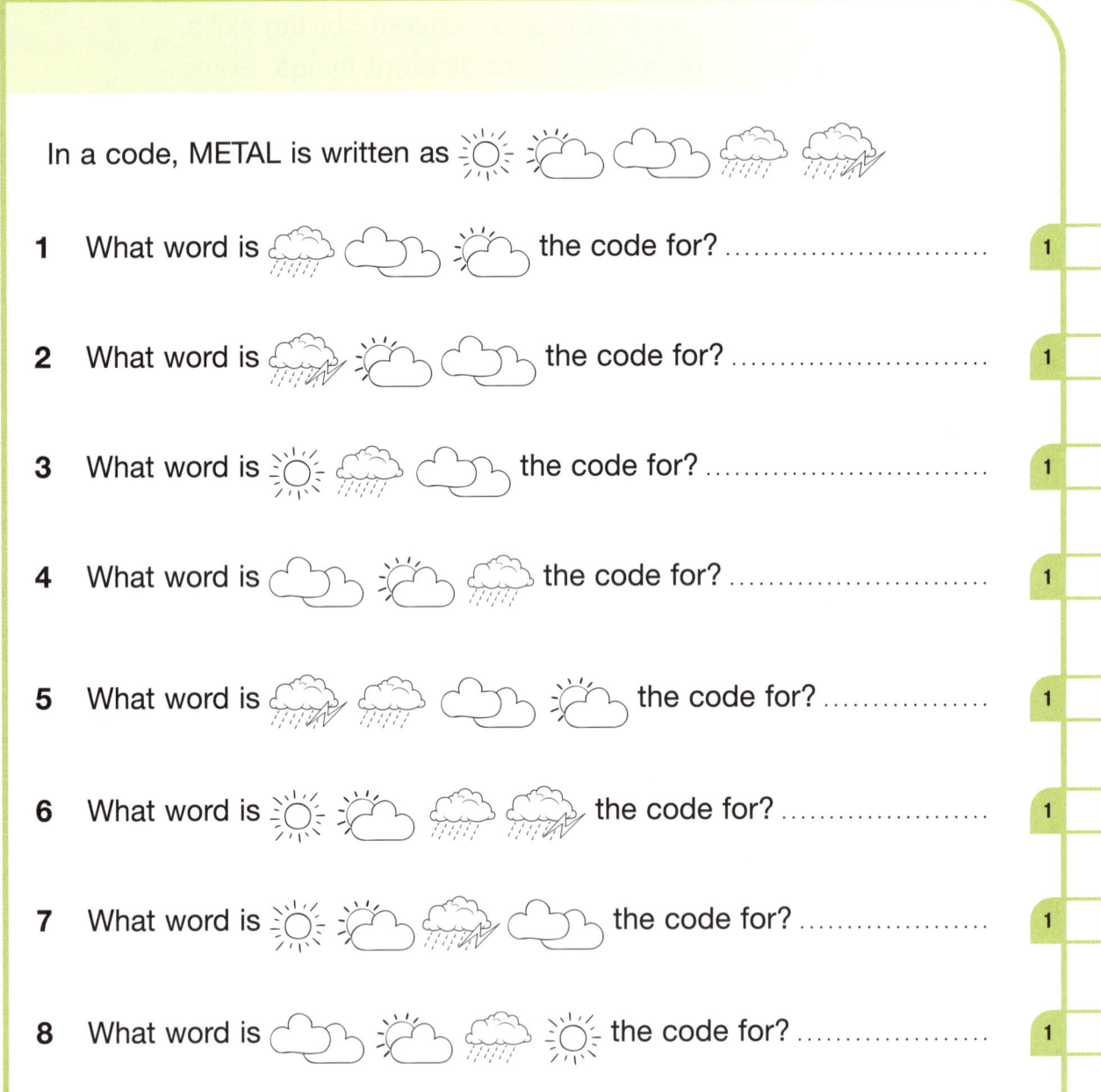

WORKED EXAMPLE

In a code, **BEAD** is written as **2514**. Use the same numbers to write the codes of the following words.

BAD ....

BED ....

ADD ....

- Each letter has been replaced by a number:
  B = 2
  E = 5
  A = 1
  D = 4
- For the word BAD, B becomes 2, A becomes 1 and D becomes 4, so the code is: 214.
- For the word BED, B becomes 2, E becomes 5 and D becomes 4, so the code is: 254.
- For the word ADD, A becomes 1 and both D's become 4, so the code is: 144.

So the answer is:
  BAD **214**
  BED **254**
  ADD **144**

Now try it yourself.

In a code, TEAM is written as 4123. Use the same numbers to write the codes of the following words.

9   MAT ....

10   MATE ....

11   MET ....

12   MEAT ....

In a code, PLANE is written as 13578. Use the same numbers to write the codes of the following words.

13 PEN ....

14 NAP ....

15 PANE ....

16 LEAN ....

WORKED EXAMPLE

If the code 32514 spells the word FLAKE, which words do the following numbers spell?

423 ....

2514 ....

2453 ....

- Each number stands for a letter:
  3 = F
  2 = L
  5 = A
  1 = K
  4 = E
- For the first code, 4 = E, 2 = L and 3 = F. This code spells the world ELF.
- For the second code, 2 = L, 5 = A, 1 = K and 4 = E. This code spells the world LAKE.
- For the final code, 2 = L, 4 = E, 5 = A and 3 = F. This code spells the word LEAF.

So the answer is:
  423 **ELF**
  2514 **LAKE**
  2453 **LEAF**

Now try it yourself!

In a code, 51342 spells the word BREAD. What do the following numbers spell?

17 532 ....

18 5342 ....

19 341 ....

20 2341 ....

In a code, 24315 spells the word THOSE. What do the following numbers spell?

21 432 ....

22 4312 ....

23 245 ....

24 4315 ....

Puzzle 1

Months and Days

KEY SKILL

These puzzles are about days of the week and months of the year. You need to look for the clues in the boxes to help you choose the right answer. Not all the clues in the boxes will need to be used. You need to pick the right ones!

WORKED EXAMPLE

Use the information shown in the boxes to help find the answer to the questions. Underline the correct answer.

| The days of the week are Monday, Tuesday, Wednesday, Thursday, Friday, Saturday and Sunday. |

| There are 31 days in May. |

| There are 30 days in June. |

1. 1st June is a Tuesday. What will be the date on the Thursday of that week?

    2nd June   3rd June   4th June

2. What is the date of the last day in May?

    25th May   30th May   31st May

Read through all the boxes and look for the information that will help.

Question 1:
One box shows the days of the week and their order:
Thursday is two days after Tuesday.
This means two days after the 1st will be the 3rd.
So the answer to the first question is 3rd June.

54

Question 2:

One box shows there are 31 days in May.
This means the last day in May will be the 31st.
So the answer to the second question is 31st May.

Now try it yourself!

> The months of the year are January, February, March, April, May, June, July, August, September, October, November and December.

> There are 52 weeks in a year.

> There are 7 days in one week.

Underline the correct answer.

1 What is the next month after July?

June August September

2 Which is the 4th month of the year?

March August April

3 How many days are in 2 weeks?

7 14 10

4 How many months are there in a year?

10 12 15

Months and Days

Puzzle 1

Months and Days

February has 28 days, except in a leap year when it has 29 days.

These months have 31 days: January, March, May, June, July, August, October and December.

There are 365 days in a normal year and 366 days in a leap year.

These months have 30 days: April, June, September and November.

A leap year happens every 4 years.

5 How many days are in February when it is a leap year?

24   28   29

6 How often does a leap year happen?

every 4 years   every 2 years   every 5 years

7 How many days does April have?

31 days   28 days   30 days

8 How many days does October have?

31 days   28 days   30 days

Total 8

Mixed Paper

Mixed Paper 1

Underline the word in the brackets <u>closest</u> in meaning to the word in capitals.

Example   SMILE   (sulk   played   <u>grin</u>)

1   CUP   (drink   plate   mug)

2   SPEAK   (listen   talk   mouth)

3   LIE   (ask   fib   cry)

Write the missing number in each sequence.

Example   5   10   15   **20**   25

4   50   40   30   10

5   10   12   14   18

6   14   12   8   6

7   3   9   12   15

8   3   5   7   11

Make a word from the letters of the alphabet. The alphabet has been written out to help.

a b c d e f g h i j k l m n o p q r s t u v w x y z

9   Make a word from the 4th, 15th and 7th letters of the alphabet.

....

10 Make a word from the 10th, 1st and 13th letters of the alphabet.

.... 1

11 Make a word from the 12th, 5th, 1st and 4th letters of the alphabet.

.... 1

Change the first word of the third pair in the same way as the other pairs to make a new word.

Example   DIG, DOG   FIG, FOG   BIG, **BOG**

12 BUG, BAG   TUG, TAG   RUG, ... 1

13 MOP, MAP   LOP, LAP   TOP, ... 1

14 RAT, RUT   CAT, CUT   BAT, ... 1

15 WAN, WIN   BAN, BIN   FAN, ... 1

16 MAN, MEN   PAN, PEN   TAN, ... 1

Underline the one word which <u>cannot be made</u> from the letters of the word in capital letters.

Example   GROWN   now   worn   <u>worm</u>   won

17 WATER   wet   ate   war   ram   1

18 MARKS   ark   mar   ram   sea   1

19 STEAM   mat   arm   set   tea   1

20 COAST   cat   cot   car   sat   1

21 SPEAK   ape   peak   seat   peas   1

Remove one letter from the word in capital letters to leave a new word. The meaning of the new word is given in the clue.

Example   AUNT   an insect   **ANT**

22 FIND   a shark has one   ....

23 MILL   not well   ....

24 BEAR   we hear with this   ....

25–27   Match one word from the group on the left with one word from the group on the right to form a new word. The word on the left always comes first.

butter   side
eye   fly
sea   lash

Example   sun + flower = sunflower

.... + ... = ...

.... + ... = ...

.... + ... = ...

If ☀ = 1, ★ = 2, ☽ = 3, ☁ = 4 and 🌈 = 5, find the sum of the following. Write your answer as a number.

Example   ☀ + ★ = **3**

28 ☀ + ☽ + 🌈 = ...

29 ★ + ☁ + ☀ + ☽ = ...

30 ☀ + ☀ + ☁ + ☁ = ...

Mixed Paper 2

Find the number the picture has replaced.

1   7 +  = 10    = ...

2   8 − (elephant) = 2   (elephant) = ...

3   (ladybird) + 9 = 14   (ladybird) = ...

4   5 × (helicopter) = 30   (helicopter) = ...

5–9

Write these words in the correct group.

| lily   star   poppy   sun   tulip |

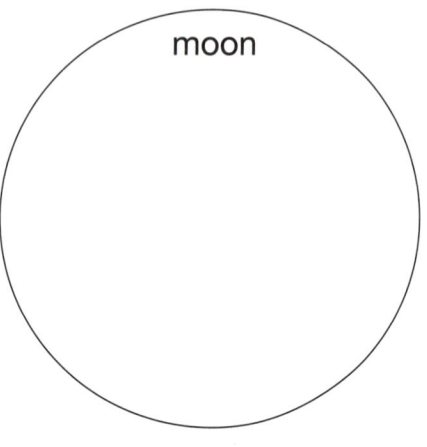 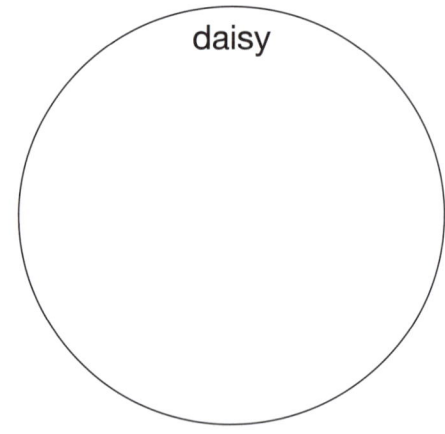

Add one letter from the list to the front of the capital letters. The sentences must make sense. Each letter can only be used once.

Example   I drink from a **C**UP.

C   D   S   P

10   We sit on ____ HAIRS.

11   My new ____ HOES are hurting my feet.

12 We will fly in a _____ LANE.

13 Can you see when it is _____ ARK?

Fill in the missing letters. The alphabet has been written out to help.

A B C D E F G H I J K L M N O P Q R S T U V W X Y Z

Example A is to B as C is to **D**

14 A is to F as C is to _____

15 B is to G as D is to _____

16 J is to L as K is to _____

17 P is to R as O is to _____

18 S is to V as W is to _____

In a code, PASTE is written as 👑 🏰 🐲 🛡 🤴.

19 What word is 🐲 🏰 🛡 the code for? ....

20 What word is 👑 🤴 🛡 the code for? ....

21 What word is 🐲 🛡 🤴 👑 the code for? ....

If the code 34125 spells the word STARE, what do the following numbers spell?

22 412 ....

23 214 ....

24 3514 ....

Change the first word into the last word by changing one letter at a time. The word in the middle must be a real word.

Example   IS → **IF** → OF

25 HE → .... → MY

26 AT → .... → IF

27 IS → .... → ON

The letters of the word in capitals have been muddled up. Put them in the correct order to make a proper word. The answer will complete the sentence sensibly.

Example   A BEZAR is an animal with stripes. **ZEBRA**

28 Please clean up the SSME you made. ....

29 I was scared the SWPA was going to sting me. ....

30 The bird had a WMOR in its beak. ....

Total 30

Mixed Paper 3

Underline the pair of words with the most similar meaning.

Example happy, angry   <u>begin, start</u>   dear, read

1 bun, plate   pen, fork   dog, puppy

2 in, shut   chum, buddy   early, shout

3 game, out   hush, go   nap, sleep

4 it, them   wet, hot   pond, lake

5 tiny, small   big, tiny   green, bread

Write the missing number in each sequence.

Example   1   12   123   **1234**

6   5   56   567   ....

7   4   45   456   ....

8   1   12   123   1234   ....

9   3   34   345   3456   ....

10   5   56   567   5678   ....

Write these words in alphabetical order. The alphabet has been written out to help.

a b c d e f g h i j k l m n o p q r s t u v w x y z

Example   truck   car   bus

(1) **bus**   (2) **car**   (3) **truck**

11   fig   log   bog

(1) ....   (2) ....   (3) ....

12   men   hen   pen

(1) ....   (2) ....   (3) ....

13   try   fly   dry

(1) ....   (2) ....   (3) ....

Change the first word into the last word by changing one letter at a time. The word in the middle must be a real word.

Example   IS → **IF** → OF

14   UP → .... → AS

15   OF → .... → IT

16   WE → .... → HI

17   US → .... → AT

18   OR → .... → IF

Underline the two words which are made from the same letters.

Example   TAP   PET   <u>TEA</u>   POT   <u>EAT</u>

19   ANT   TON   TEN   TIN   TAN

20   ARE   APE   ACE   PEA   AND

21   OWE   WIN   NOW   OWN   NEW

22   CAT   COT   TOP   ACT   CAP

23   BUN   BUT   CUB   CUT   TUB

24   Half of 👁 is 8   👁 = ...

25   3 and 🙂 is 20 altogether   🙂 = ...

26   Double 🐯 is 24   🐯 = ...

27–30

Draw lines to match the pairs of words that have the most similar meaning.

damp   pull
tug   pale
street   wet
light   road

TOP TIP!

Always check to see if the questions asks to find the similar meaning or the opposite meaning!

Mixed Paper 4

If = 1, = 2, = 3 and = 4, find the sum of the following. Write your answer as a number.

Example  = **3**

1  = ...

2 = ...

3  = ...

Match the second pair of words in the same way as the first pair. Underline the correct word in the brackets.

Example HAND is to ARM as FOOT is to (HEAD, FINGER, **LEG**).

4 TOMATO is to RED as BANANA is to (BLUE, PURPLE, YELLOW).

5 WRITE is to PEN as PAINT is to (PAPER, BRUSH, PENCIL).

6 TIRED is to SLEEP as HUNGRY is to (LIGHT, EAT, SAD).

Remove one letter from the word in capital letters to leave a new word. The meaning of the new word is given in the clue.

Example AUNT an insect **ANT**

7 COLD not young ....

8 BIND we put rubbish in it ....

9 HURT a type of shed ....

Find and underline the two words which need to change places for each sentence to make sense.

Example She went to <u>letter</u> the <u>write</u>.

10 The east rises in the sun.

11 Let's wash up the now dishes.

12 The teacher asked the class be to quiet.

13 Everybody football to play loves.

14 I helped my brother carry the steps up the bags.

In a code, DIAL is written as 3412. Use the same numbers to write the codes of the following words.

15 DID ....

16 LAD ....

17 LID ....

Add one letter from the list to the end of the first word and start the second word. Each letter can only be used once.

Example fro (**g**) rass

k   d   e

18 win (____) eep

19 ban (____) it

20 not (____) nd

In a code, HEATS is written as 🐵🐸🦊🐻🐼

21 What word is 🐵🦊🐻 the code for? ....

22 What word is 🦊🐻🐸 the code for? ....

23 What word is 🐼🐵🐸 the code for? ....

Write the missing number in each sequence.

Example   5   10   15   **20**   25

24   10   20   40   50

25   0   5   10   15   25

26   20   18   16   12

27   9   12   15   21

Add one letter from the list to the front of the capital letters.
The sentences must make sense. Each letter can only be used once.

Example   I drink from a **C**UP.

F   H   T

28 My friend has long blond ___AIR.

29 You have a ___HUMB on each hand.

30 ___ISH swim in the sea.

Total **30**

Mixed Paper 5

Give the next two letters in each sequence. The alphabet has been written out to help.

a b c d e f g h i j k l m n o p q r s t u v w x y z

Example   cd   ce   cf   **cg**

1 ef   eg   eh   ....

2 gh   gi   gj   ....

3 tu   tv   tw   ....

4 bd   be   bf   ....

5 dd   de   df   ....

Underline one word from the brackets so that the sentences make sense.

Example   The (car, <u>cow</u>, table) was eating grass.

TOP TIP!
If there is a sentence, always read the whole of it first to get an idea of what it is about. Then use the clues in the sentence to help choose the right answer.

6 The (pony, boy, car) was reading a book.

7 The (bus, bud, cow) arrived late.

8 The (fox, train, driver) was in the car.

Add one letter from the list to the end of the first word and start the second word. Each letter can only be used once.

Example   fro (**g**) rass

> e   l   h   d

9   rea (___) irt

10 blu (___) ggs

11 hal (___) ost

12 rus (___) arm

The letters of the word in capitals have been muddled up. Put them in the correct order to make a proper word. The answer will complete the sentence sensibly.

Example   A BEZAR is an animal with stripes.   **ZEBRA**

13 The EBE buzzed as it flew away. ....

14 Can you show me the YWA? ....

15 I can ETI my laces. ....

16 We AST in the back of the car. ....

17–19

Match one word from the group on the left with one word from the group on the right to form a new word. The word on the left always comes first.

> door   bike
> week   way
> motor   end

Example   sun + flower = sunflower

.... + ... = ...

.... + ... = ...

.... + ... = ...

In a code, PLEAT is written as 45678. Use the same numbers to write the codes of the following words.

20 EAT ....

21 TEA ....

22 TALE ....

23 PLATE ....

Make a word from the letters of the alphabet. The alphabet has been written out to help.

a b c d e f g h i j k l m n o p q r s t u v w x y z

24 What word is made from the 12th, 1st, 11th and 5th letters?

....

25 What word is made from the 2nd, 5th, 1st and 11th letters?

....

26 What word is made from the 7th, 18th, 9th and 14th letters?

....

Match the second pair of words in the same way as the first pair. Underline the correct word in the brackets.

Example   HAND is to ARM as FOOT is to (HEAD, FINGER, <u>LEG</u>).

27 SIGHT is to EYES as HEARING is to (PICTURE, NOISE, EARS).

28 BIRD is to SKY as FISH is to (SAND, EARTH, WATER).

29 GRASS is to LAWN as SAND is to (BEACH, SEA, HILLS).

30 FUR is to RABBIT as SCALES are to (FISH, BIRD, HAIR).

Total 30

Mixed Paper 6

1 Double  is 8    = ... 1

2 Half of (saxophone) is 5   (saxophone) = ... 1

3 The total of 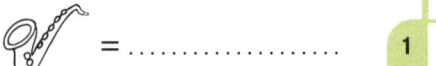 and 6 is 14   = ... 1

4 (apple) + 10 is 17 altogether    = ... 1

Underline the two words which are the odd ones out in the following groups of words.

| **Example** | house | black | king | purple | green |

5 hop   talk   jump   skip   speak

6 pen   table   pencil   chair   sofa

7 book   fork   spoon   paper   knife

8 sing   ball   talk   bull   shout

9–12

Choose a word from the list that can be put in front of each of the following words to form new words.

Example <u>sun</u>shine   <u>sun</u>burn

<u>sun</u>set   <u>sun</u>glasses

| pen | hat | sea | ship |

.... shell

.... shore

.... food

.... side

In a code, 45213 spells the word SWING, what do the following numbers spell?

13 521 ....

14 523 ....

15 52134 ....

Write these words in alphabetical order. The alphabet has been written out to help.

| a b c d e f g h i j k l m n o p q r s t u v w x y z |

Example truck   car   bus

(1) <u>bus</u>   (2) <u>car</u>   (3) <u>truck</u>

16 hut   pot   cut

(1) .... (2) .... (3) ....

17 ant   eve   bee

(1) ....   (2) ....   (3) ....

18 sea   ate   fun

(1) ....   (2) ....   (3) ....

Underline the word in the brackets <u>opposite</u> in meaning to the word in capitals.

Example   SMALL   (tiny   <u>large</u>   wide)

19 CLOSE   (glue   open   shut)

20 GO   (leave   exit   arrive)

21 GIVE   (gift   make   take)

22 HEAT   (freeze   warm   cook)

23 HIGH   (low   tall   flat)

Underline one word from the brackets so that the sentences make sense.

Example   The (car, <u>cow</u>, table) was eating grass.

24 The (snow, sun, wind) was white on the ground.

25 The window was made of (bricks, glass, tiles).

26 The boy read the (button, cloth, book).

Change the first word of the third pair in the same way as the other pairs to give a new word.

Example   DIG, DOG   FIG, FOG   BIG, **BOG**

27 VAT, VET   PAT, PET   SAT, ...

28 SOP, SUP   COP, CUP   POP, ...

29 WIN, WON   TIN, TON   SIN, ...

30 BAY, BOY   HAY, HOY   JAY, ...

Puzzle 2

Using Clues

KEY SKILL

In these types of puzzles, the goal is to use the clues in the sentences to help find the answer. Be a detective! Make sure to read the whole question and the information shown first. This will help:

- get an idea of what it is about
- see what information you have been given to find the answer.

The following are some children's favourite things to do.

Which one did most children like? ....

Linda likes den building and making comic books.

Callum likes singing and making comic books.

Ola likes den building and playing computer games.

Zara likes singing and making comic books.

den building	making comic books	singing	playing computer games
Linda Ola	Linda Callum Zara	Callum Zara	Ola

- Read through all the sentences first to get an idea of what the question is about.
- Then go back to the first sentence: 'Linda likes den building and making comic books.' Write Linda's name on the table, underneath den building and making comic books.
- Then read the second sentence again: Callum likes singing and making comic books. Write Callum's name on the table, underneath singing and making comic books.
- Do the same for the last two sentences.

- Look for the group that has the most names to find the one most children like.

The activity that has the most names is 'making comic books', so the answer is:

Which one did most children like? **making comic books**

Now try it yourself!

1–8 The following are the animals that some children own.

Which type of animal did most children own? ....

Chris had a cat and a dog.

Eva had a dog and a rabbit.

Thea had a hamster and a cat.

Param had a rabbit and a dog.

cat	dog	rabbit	hamster

9–16 The following are the favourite colours of some children.

Which colour did most children like? ....

Maisie's favourite colours are green and yellow.

Jenny's favourite colours are blue and green.

Zach's favourite colours are pink and blue.

Jakob's favourite colours are blue and yellow.

green	yellow	blue	pink